ISBN-13;978-1542952675

Printed in The United States of America

Welcome Coloring Artist to

The Outstanding Letter O

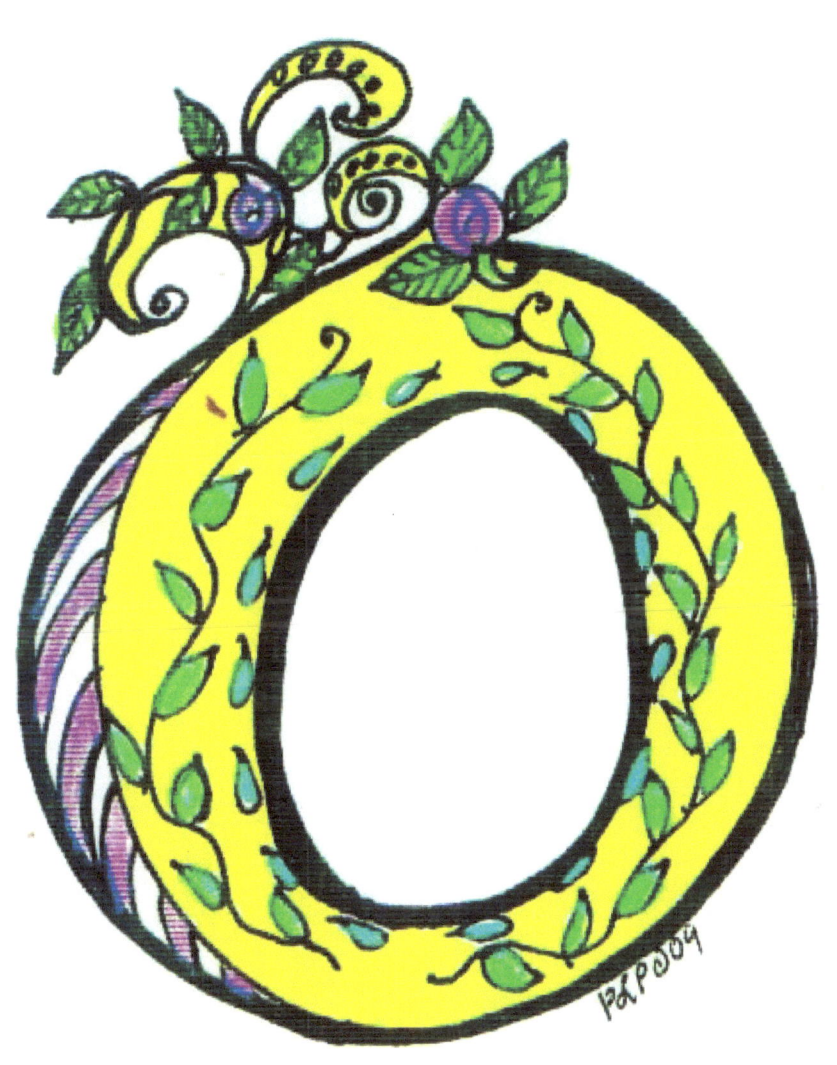

The Outstanding Letter O

Coloring Book

By Peggy Louise Parrish

C 2017

Welcome to a Coloring Adventure with the Letter O. Artist Peggy Louise Parrish has over 20 different O letters for you to color however you like. You may look at her examples for ideas or color them entirely different.

Perhaps your first or last name starts with the Letter O. Or perhaps you would simply like to tackle new ways to color all the capital letters. Creative ways of coloring are needed for creative letters. Hopefully you will make discoveries along the way. Quality colored pencils are preferred by most. If you would rather try watercolor pencils, gel pens, markers or paints be sure to place a scrap paper under your page while coloring it.

You may come up with many new ideas of O letters of your own. Above all else, enjoy the coloring journey. If you want further books of other alphabet letters they are available.

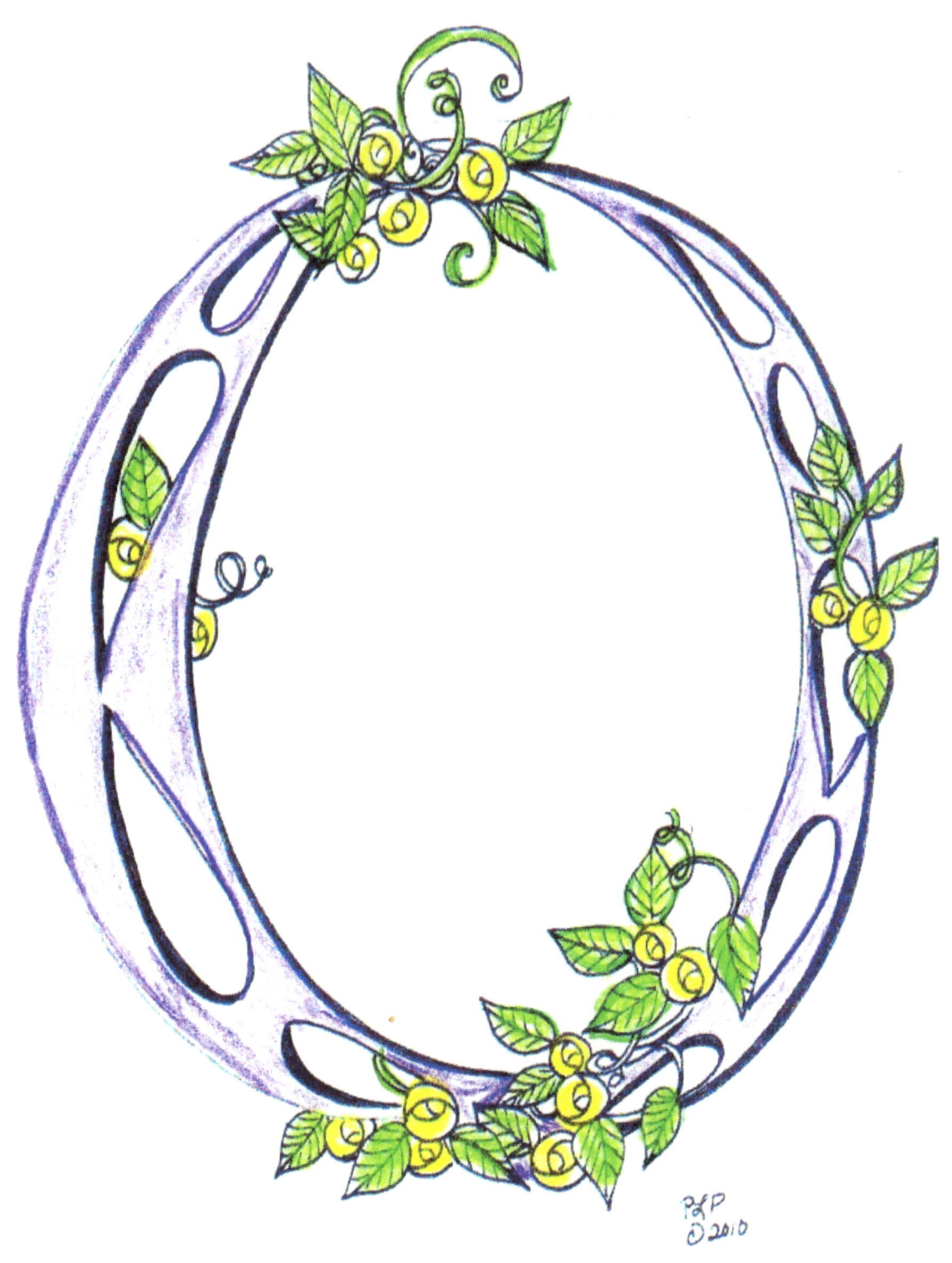

8

How would you color the rest of this?

PLP c.

Choose To Color?

11

13

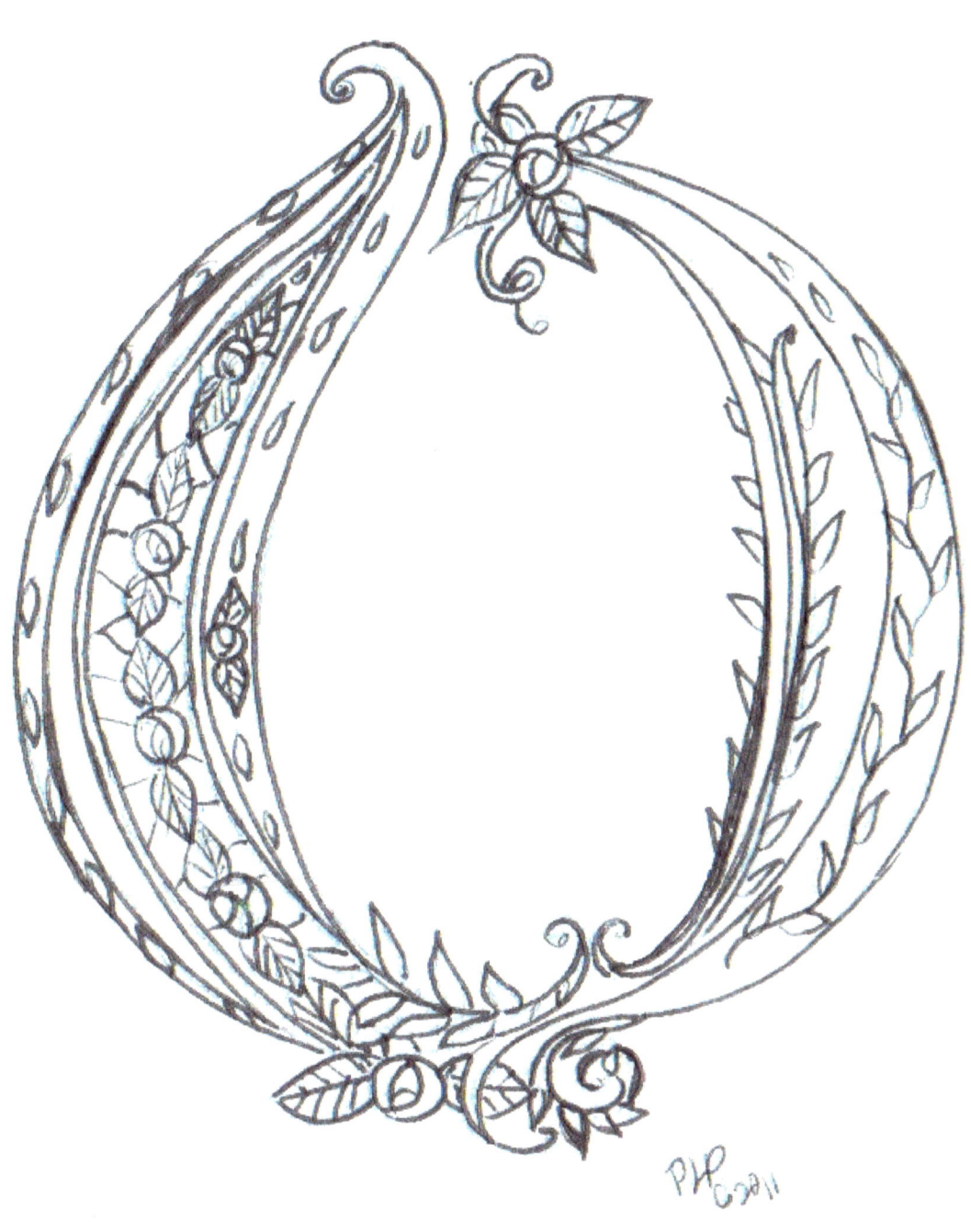

15

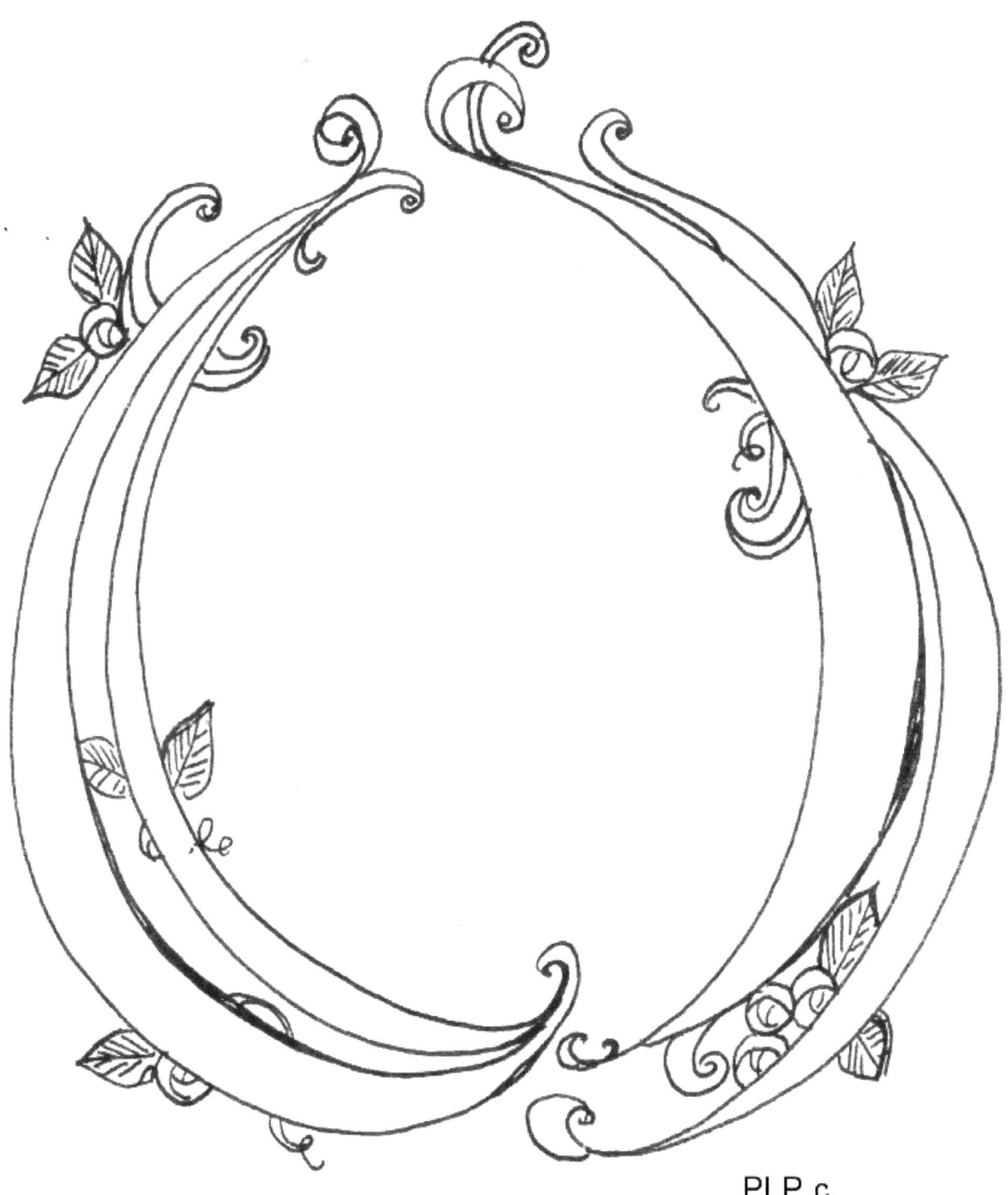

PLP c.

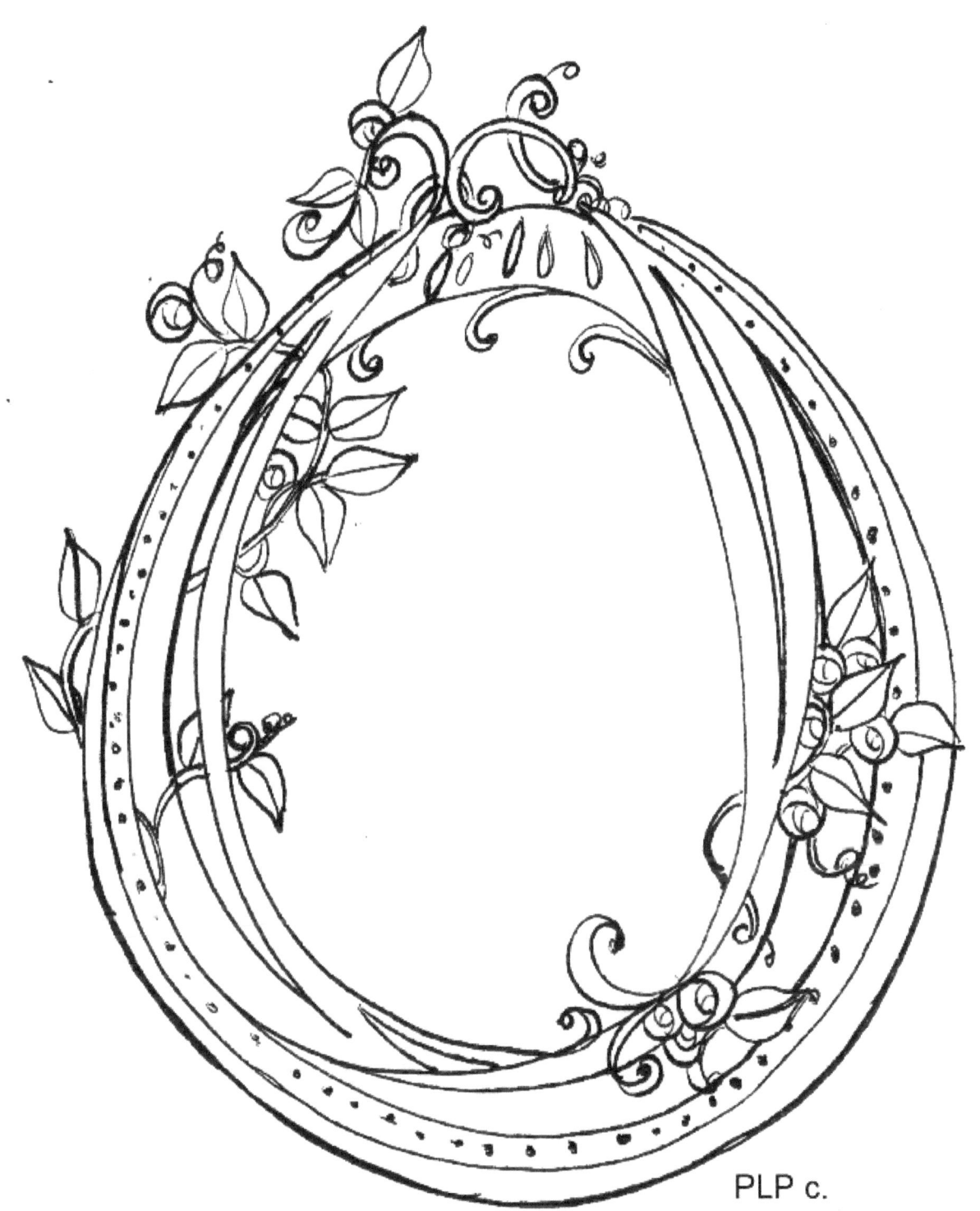

PLP c.

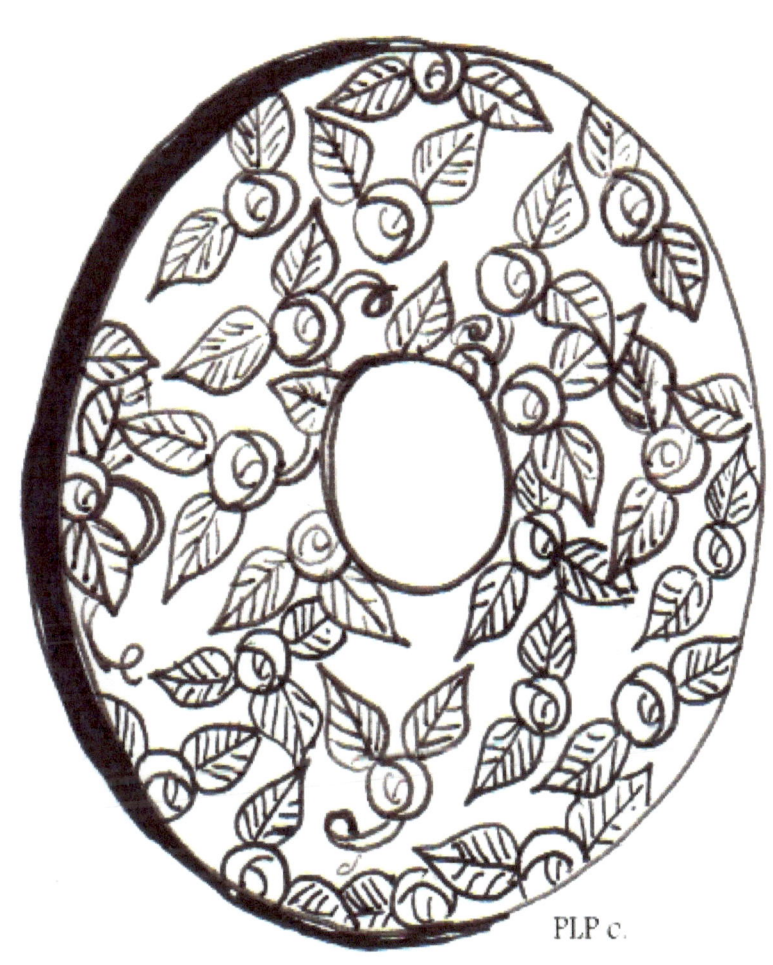

PLP c.

21

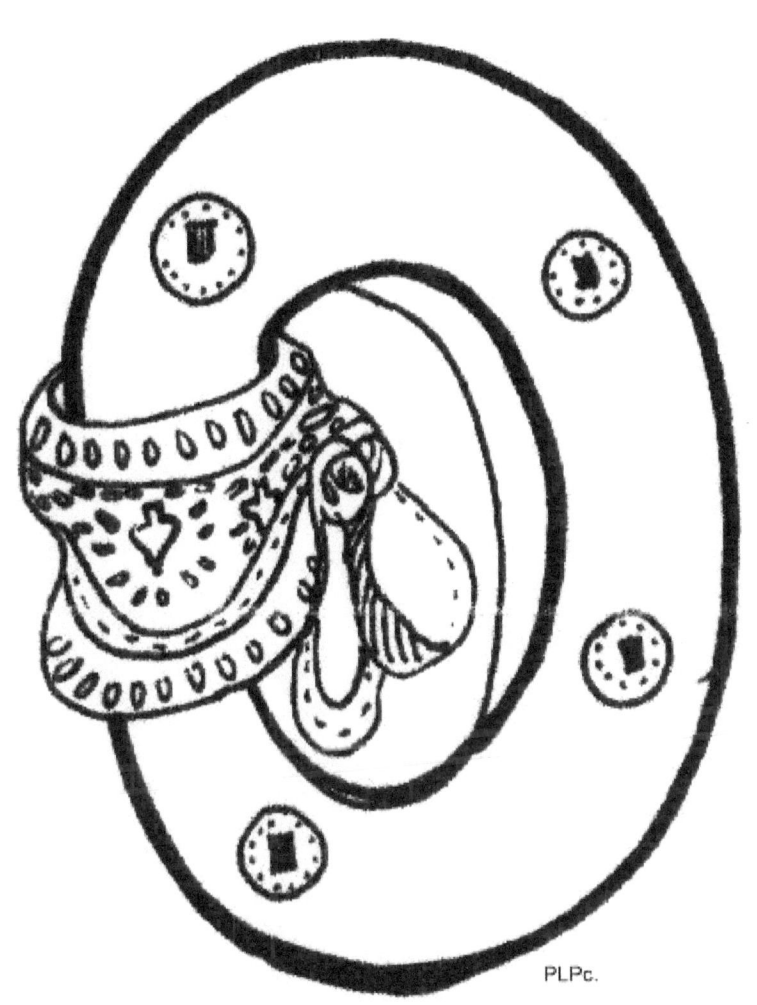

PLPc.

23

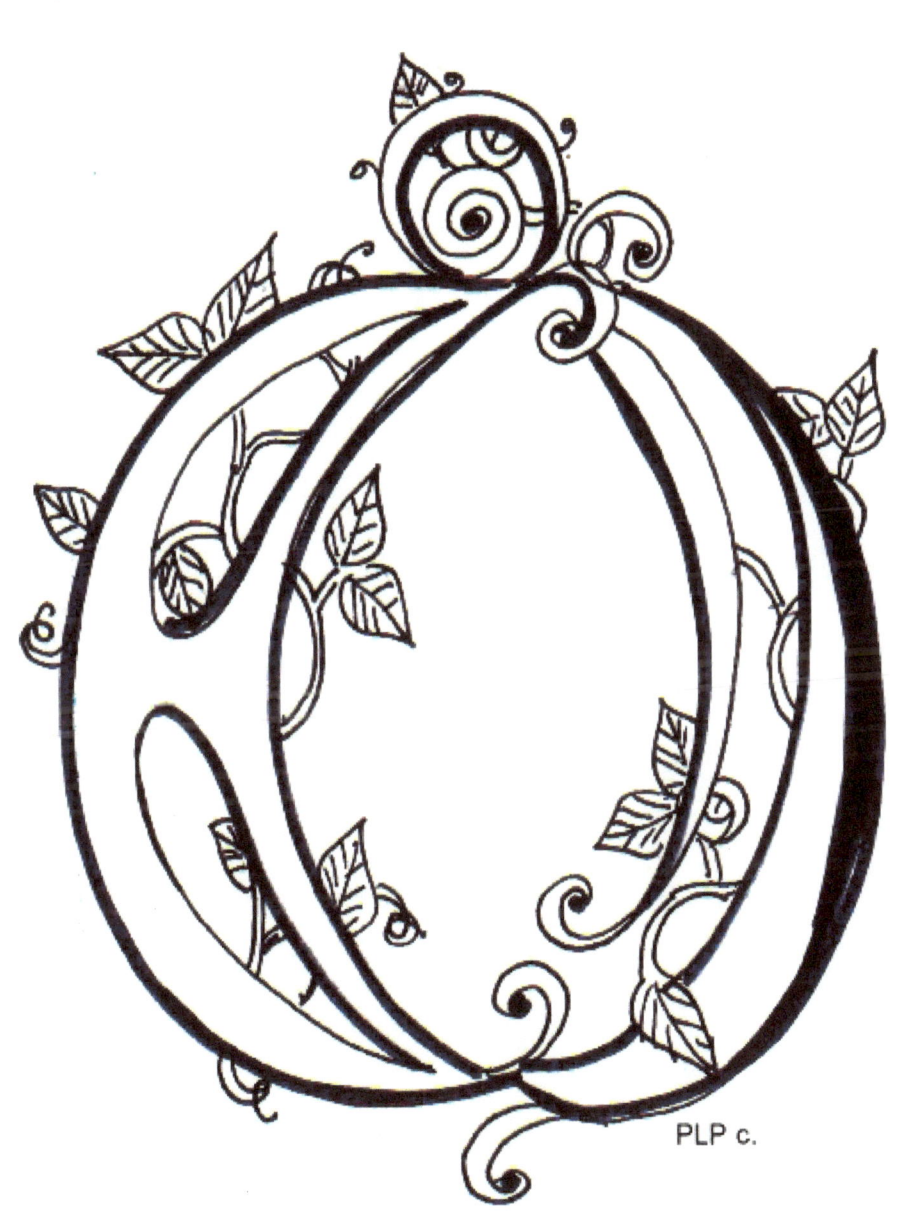

PLP c.

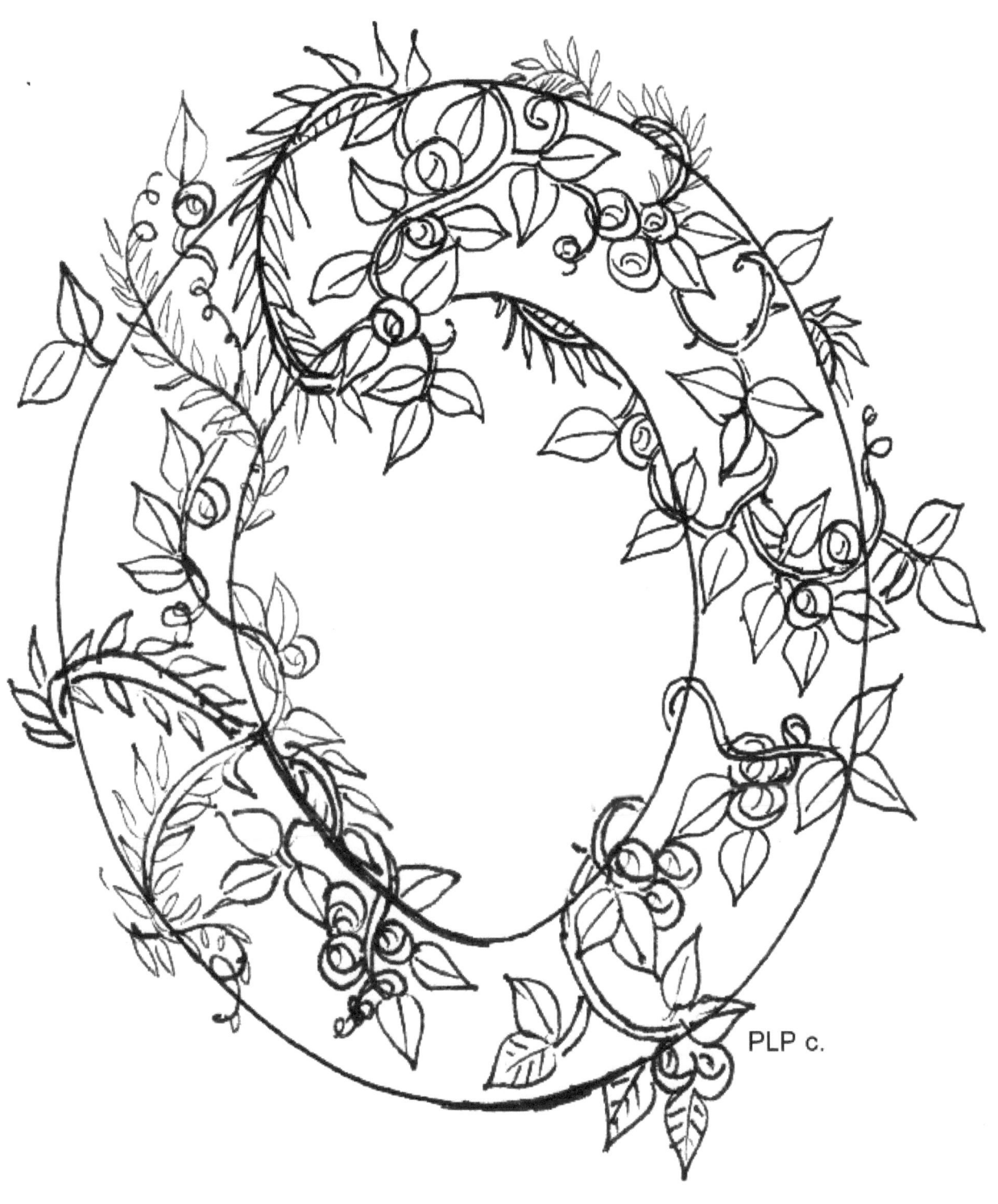

PLP c.

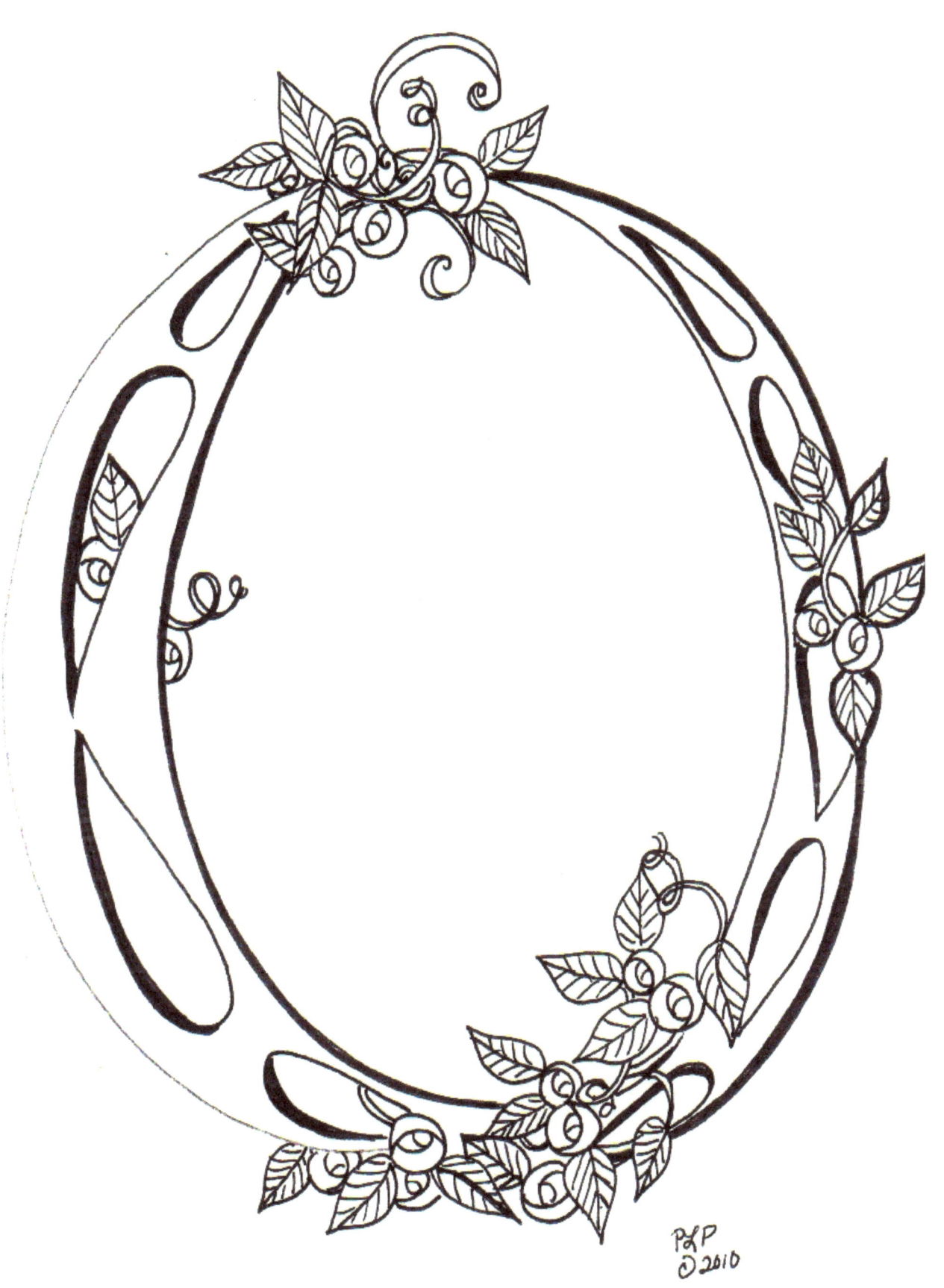

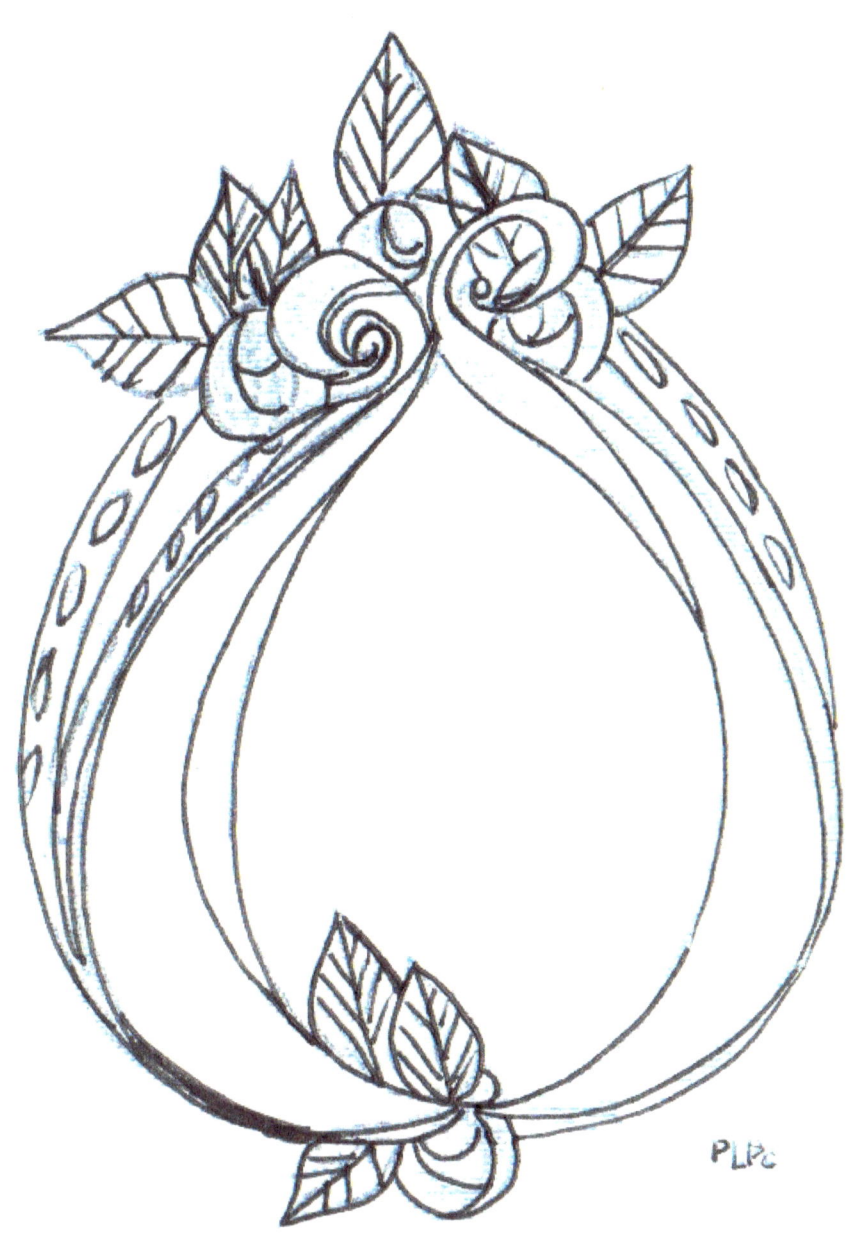

PLPc

31

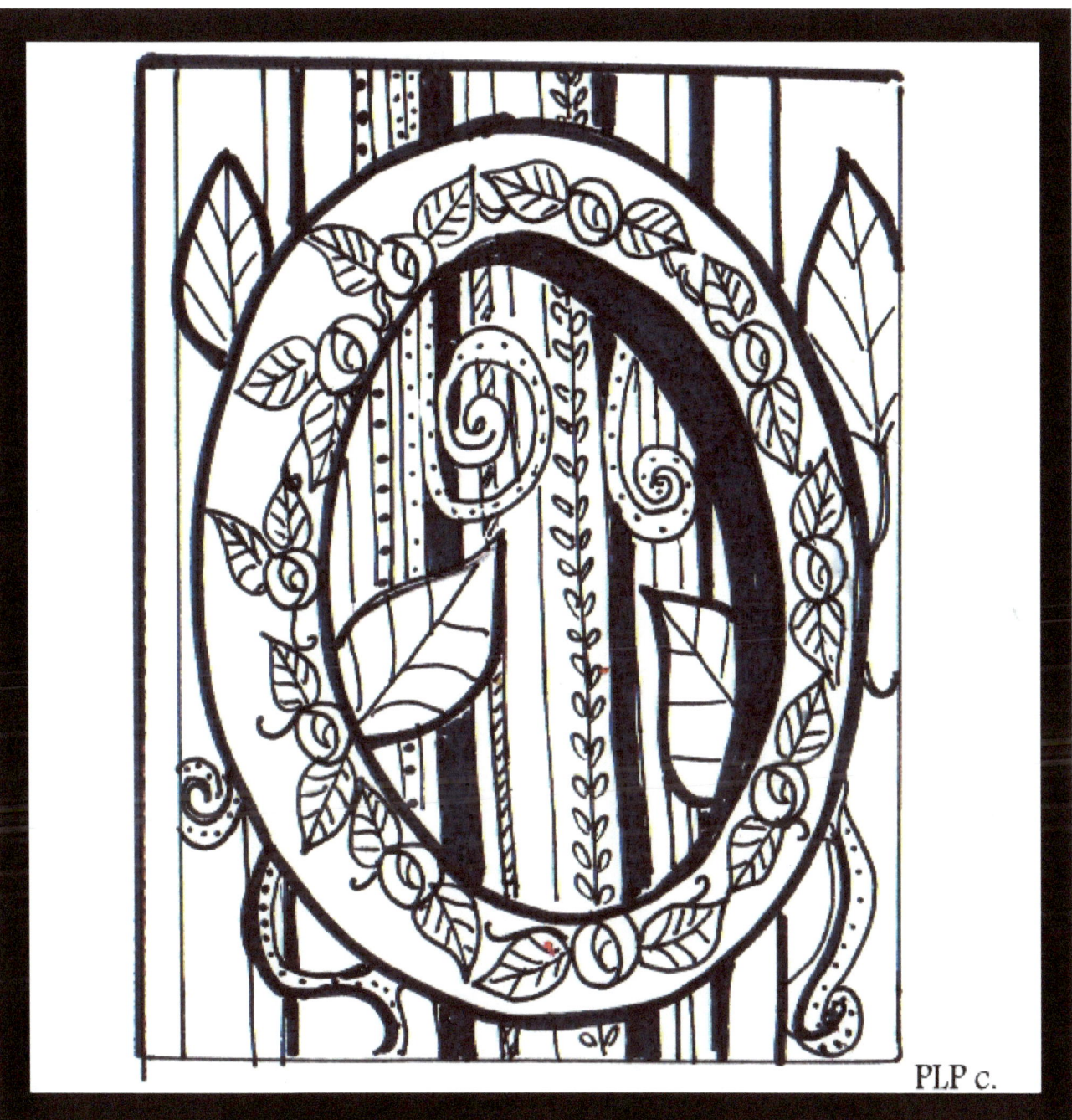

PLP c.

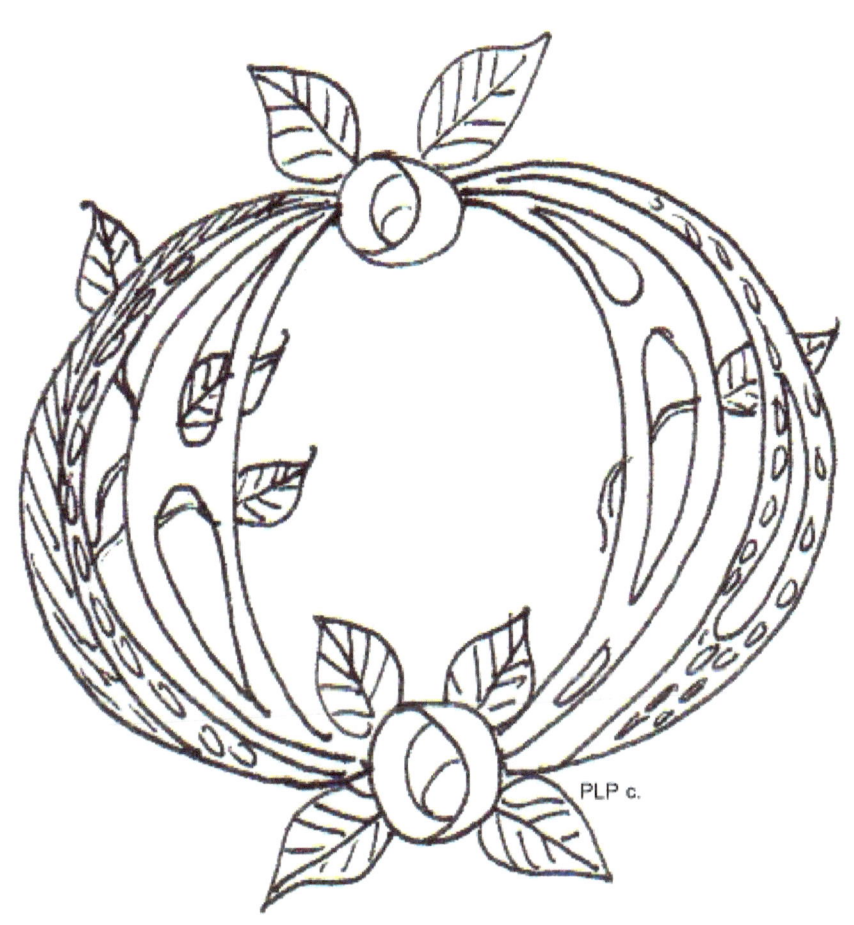

PLP c.

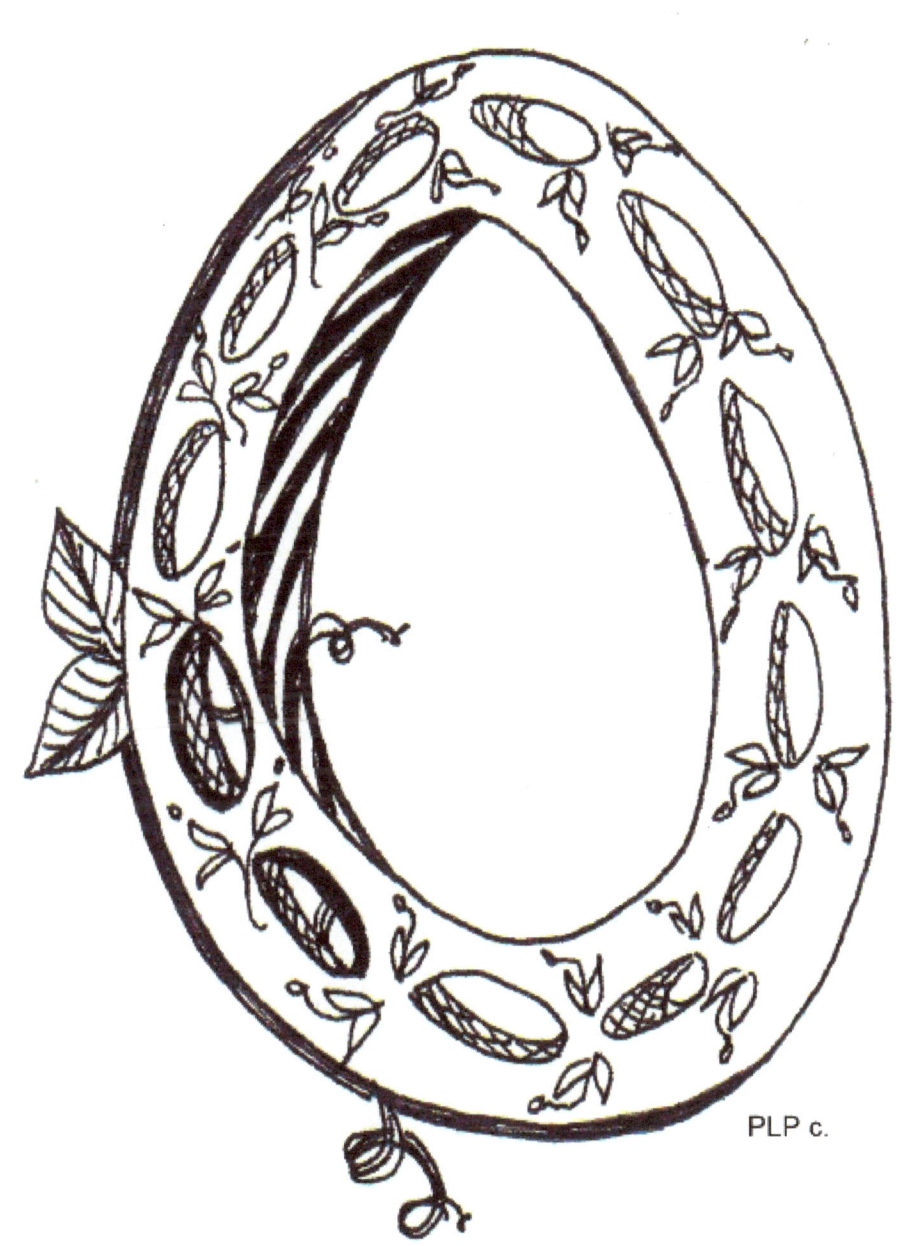

PLP c.

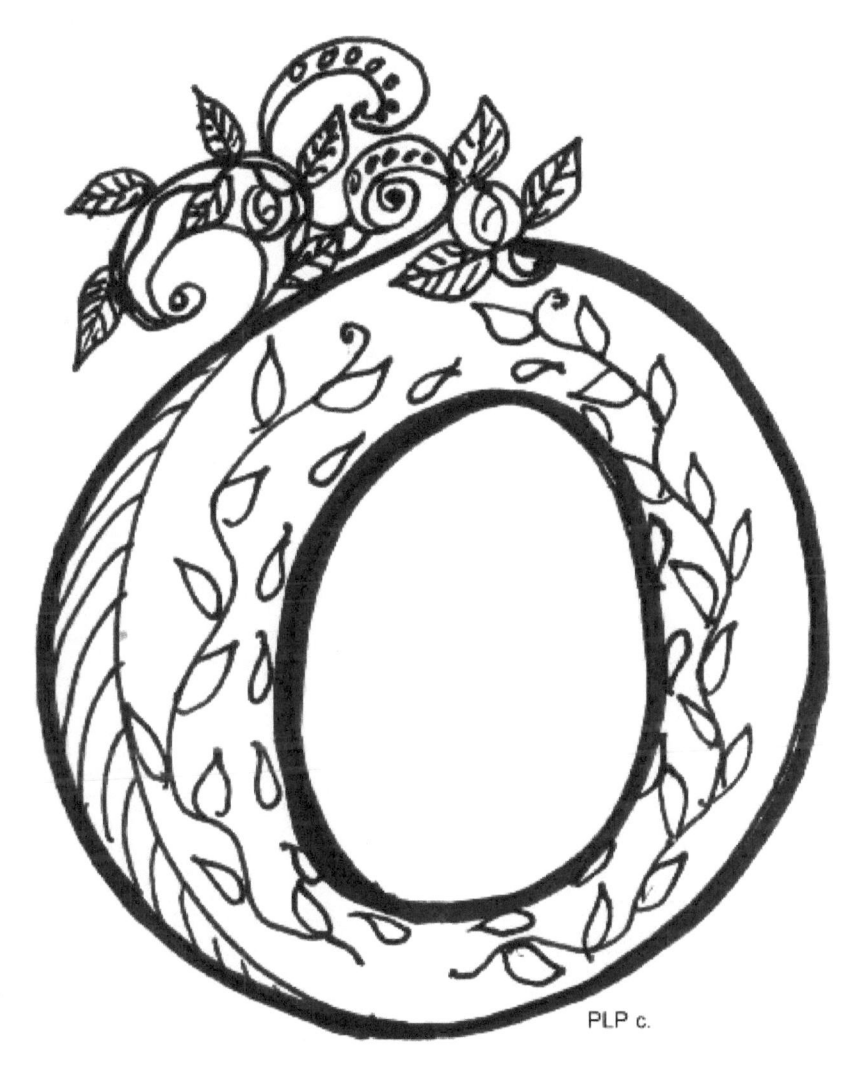

PLP c.

39

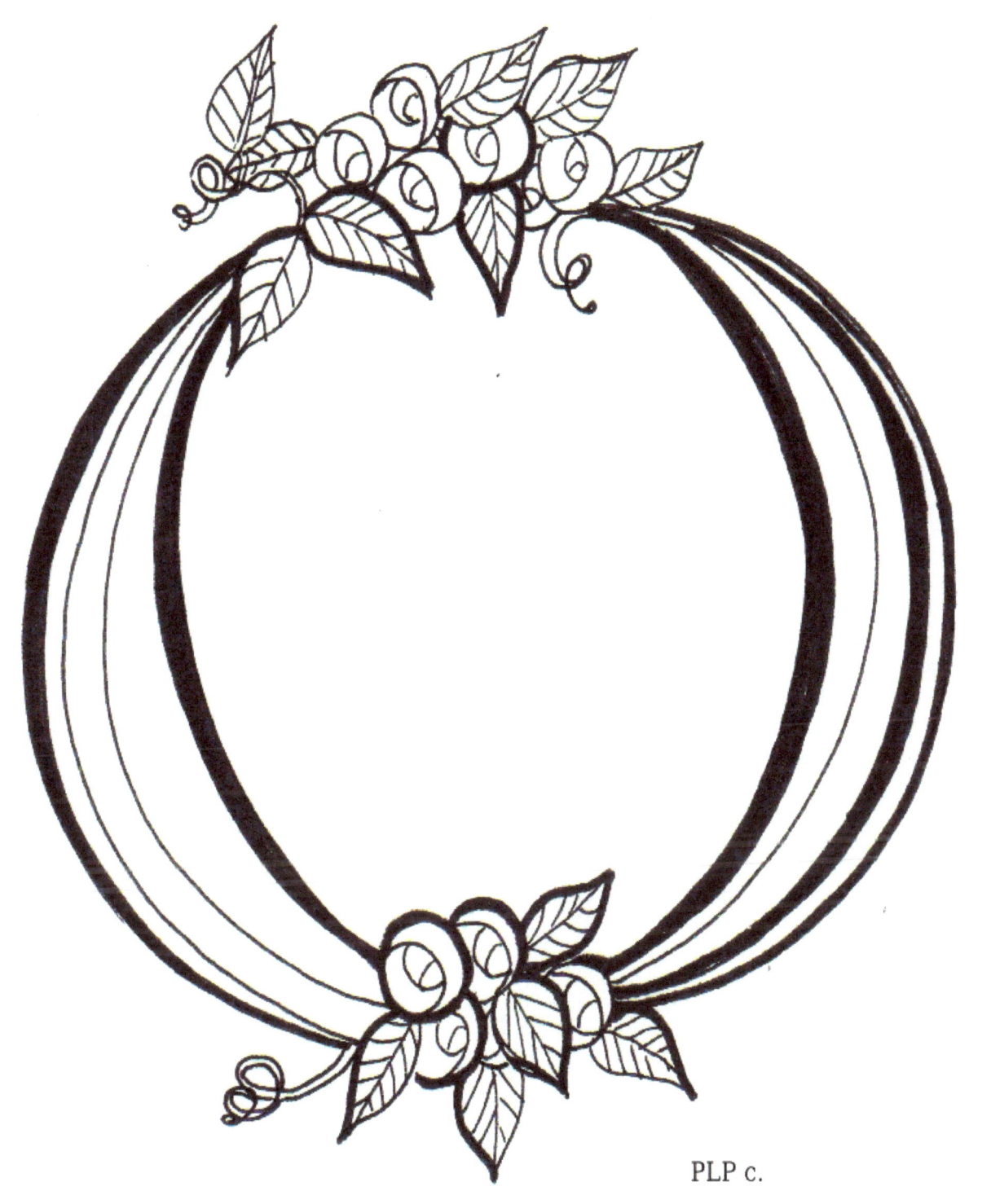

PLP c.

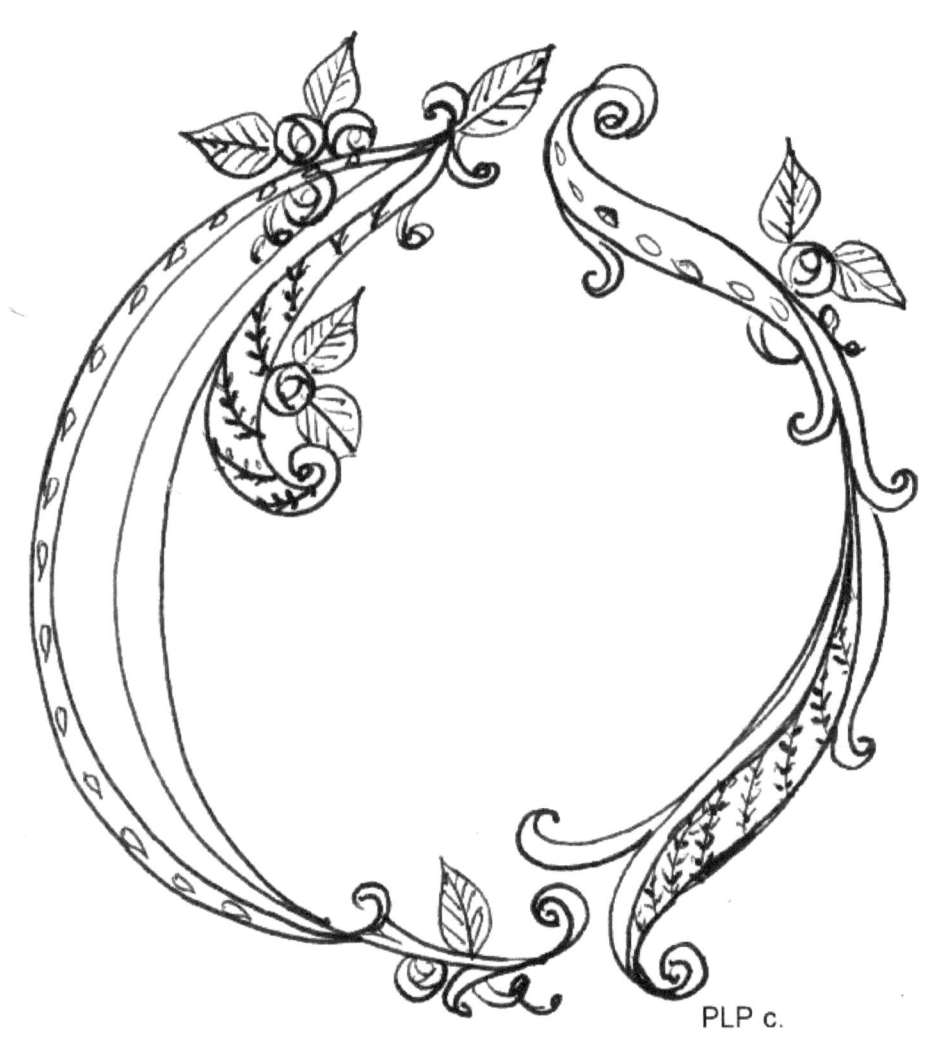

PLP c.

PLP c.

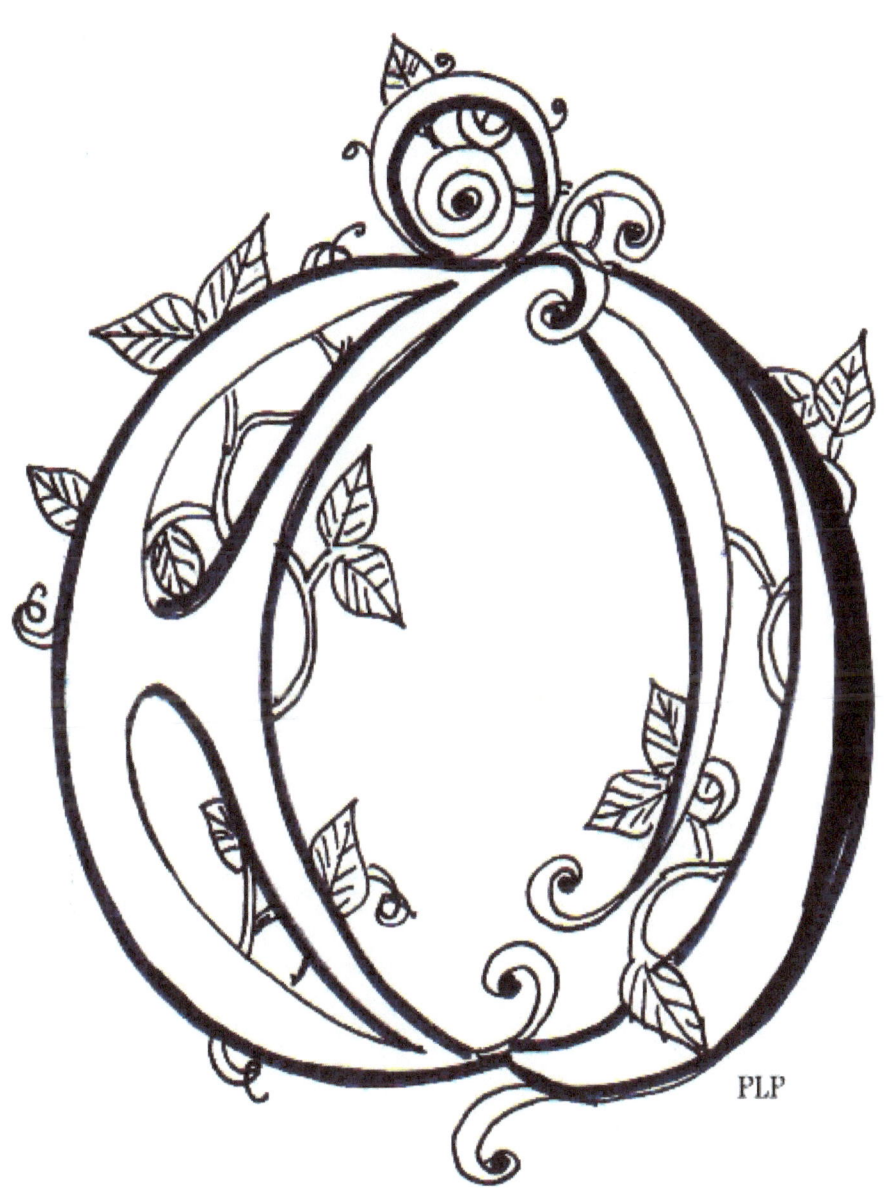

PLP

47

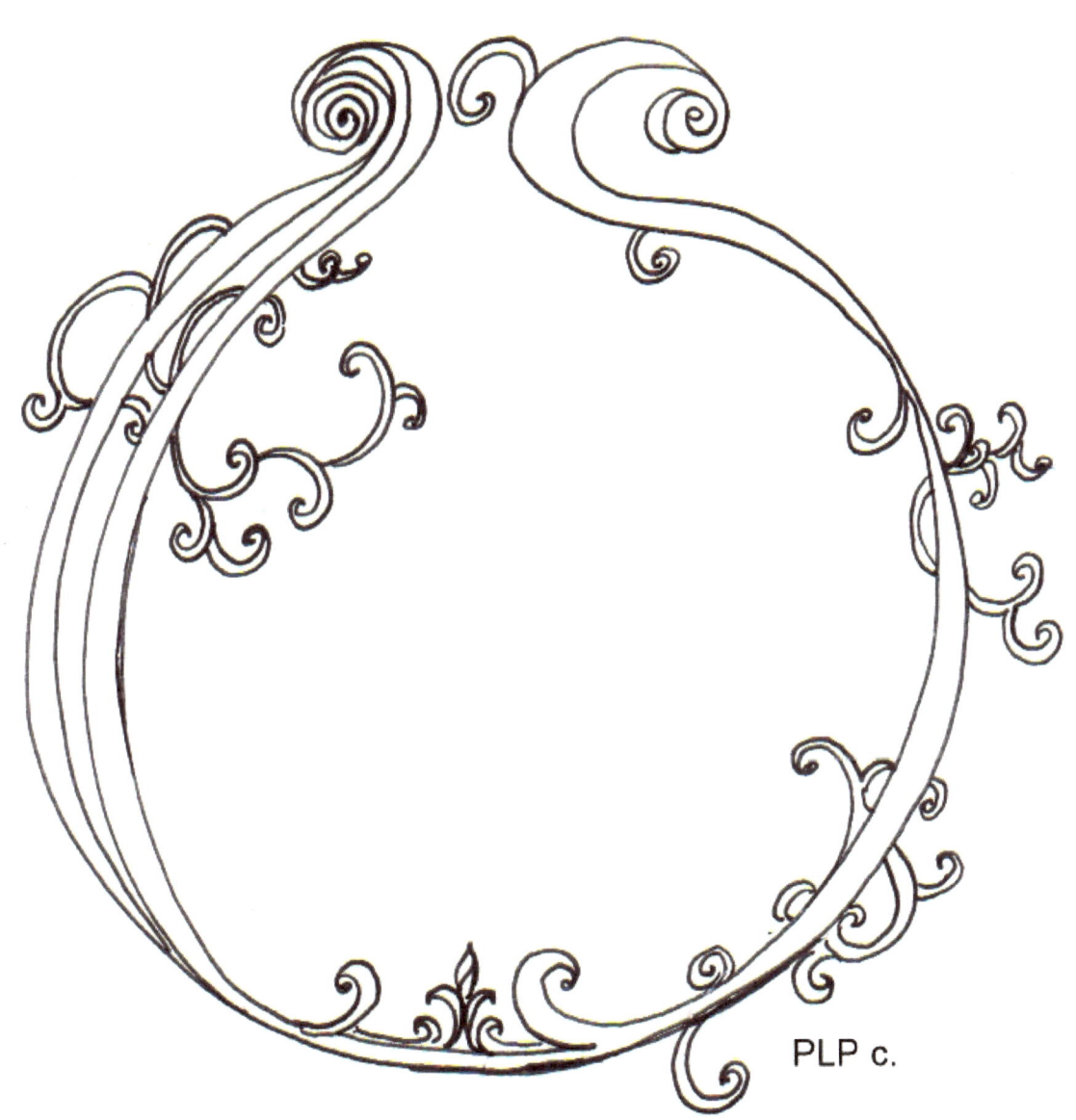

PLP c.

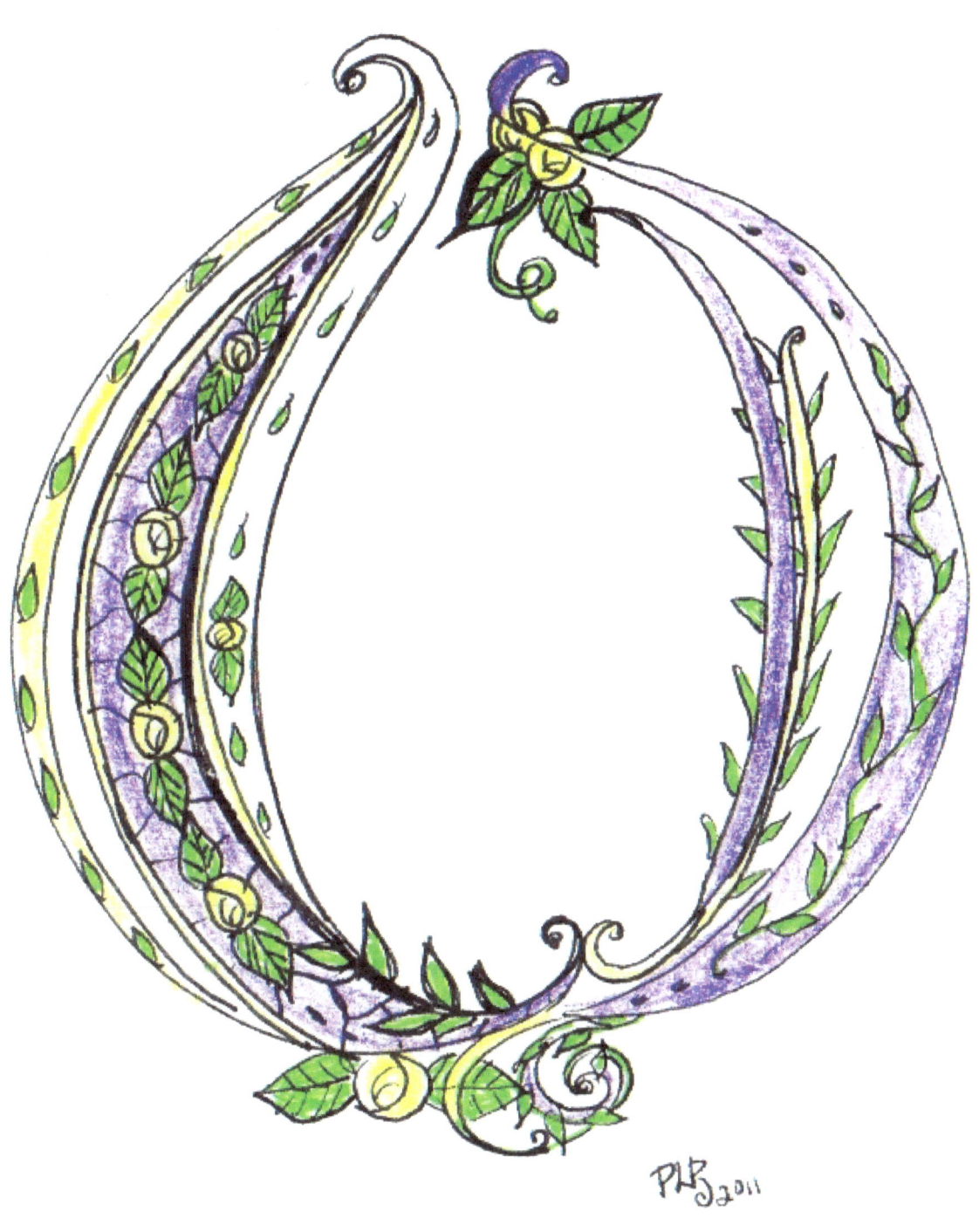

51

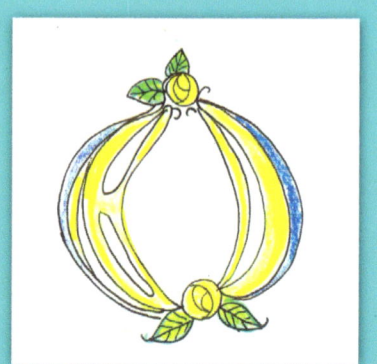
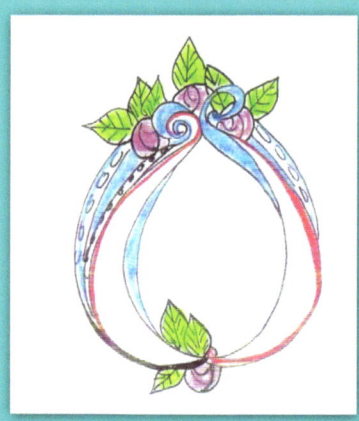
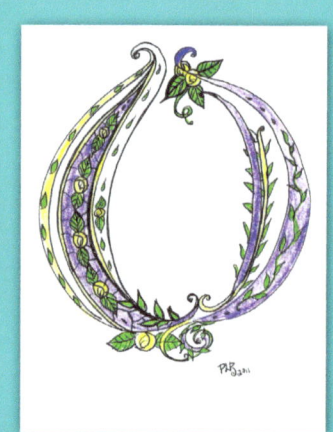
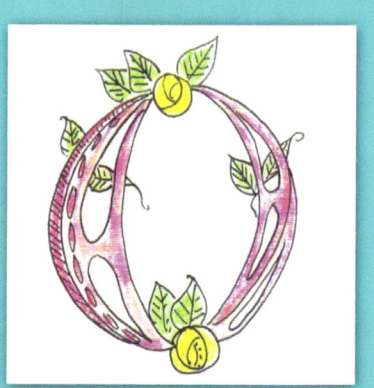
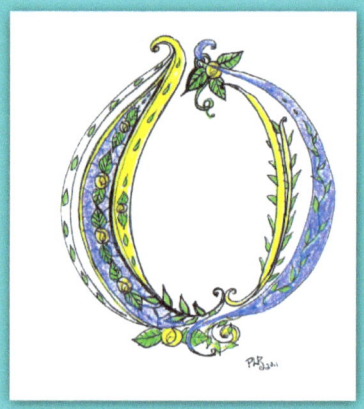
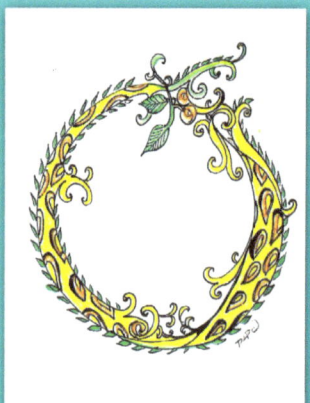
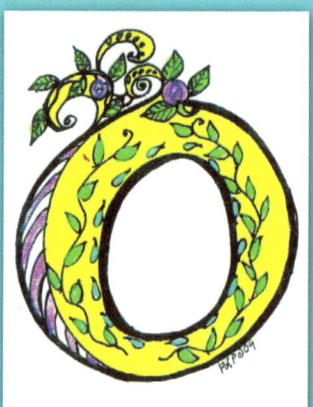

Oh how much fun the Letter O can be.

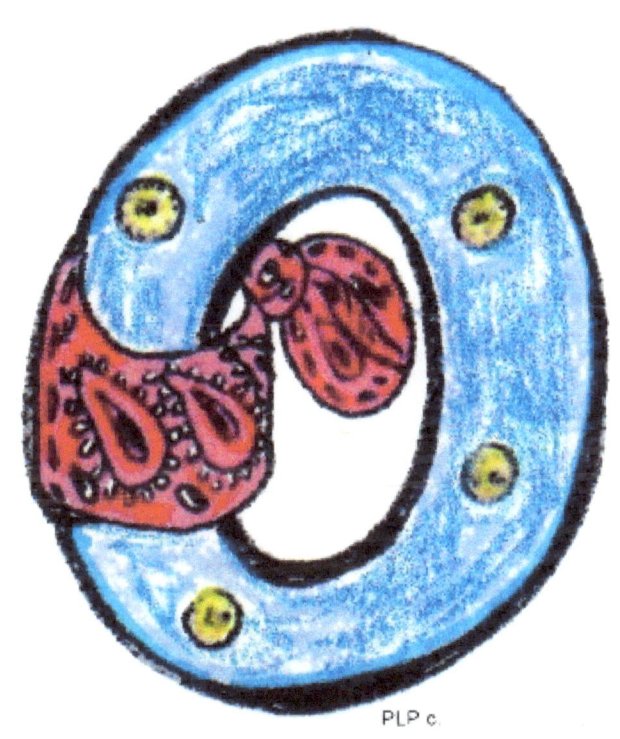

An O can be formed with all sorts of themes and beauty as well.

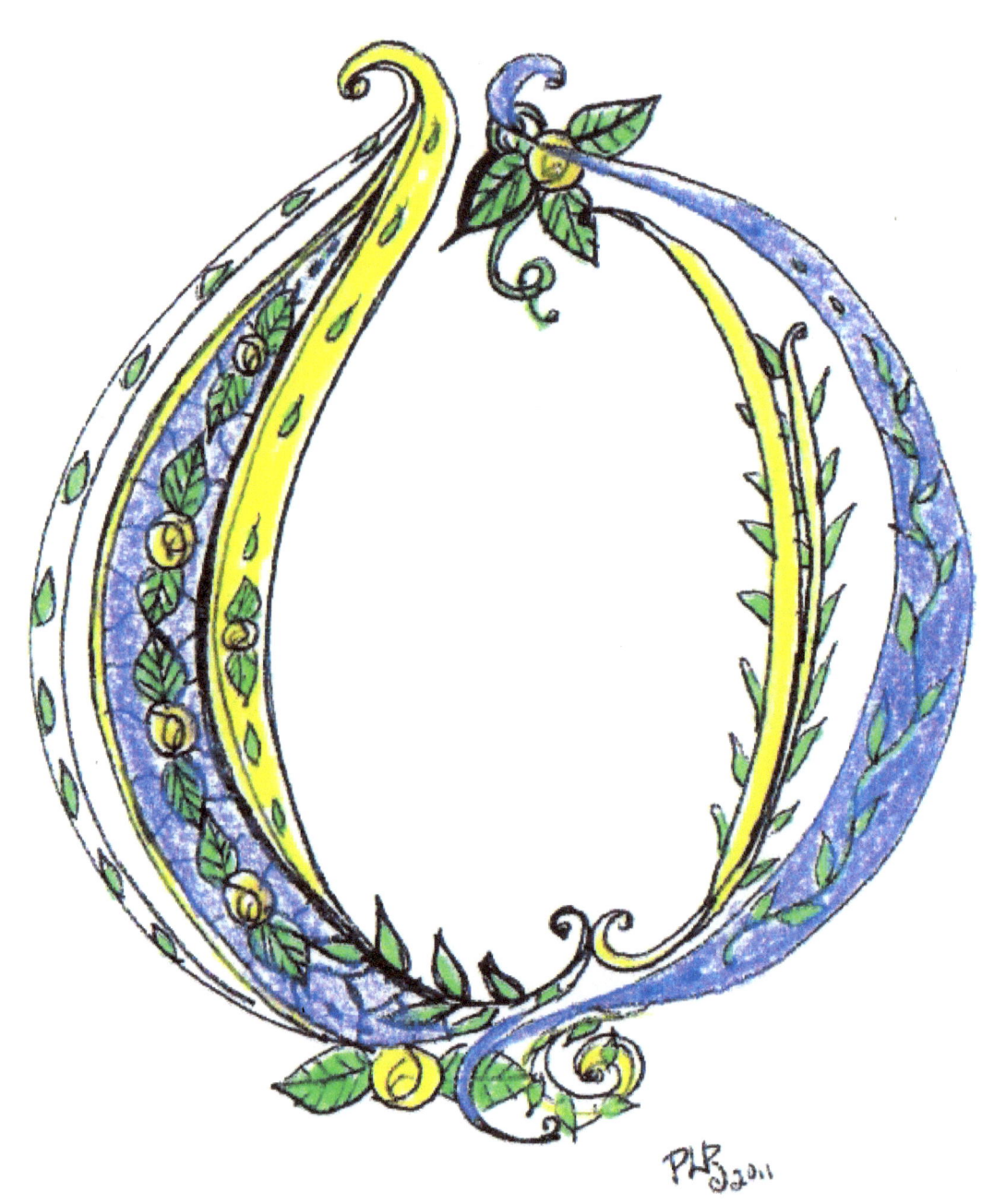

Can you make a new and creative O on this last page?

Enjoy the Letter O.....whenever you get the chance! Thanks for joining me with Letter Wonders.

Peggy Louise Parrish

www.ingramcontent.com/pod-product-compliance
Lightning Source LLC
Chambersburg PA
CBHW051055180526
45172CB00002B/643